My name is

_____

I am _____ years old

and in _____ grade

My best friend is

_____

I live in America: yes   no

I have lived here for _____

Sleeping Bear Press˙

315 E. Eisenhower Parkway, Suite 200
Ann Arbor MI 48108
www.sleepingbearpress.com

Sleeping Bear Press is an imprint of Gale, a part of Cengage Learning.

10 9 8 7 6 5 4 3 2 1

ISBN 978-1-58536-171-7

Printed by China Translation & Printing Services Limited,
Guangdong Province, China. 1st printing.   03/2011

Diary of an American Kid

Artwork by Cyd Moore

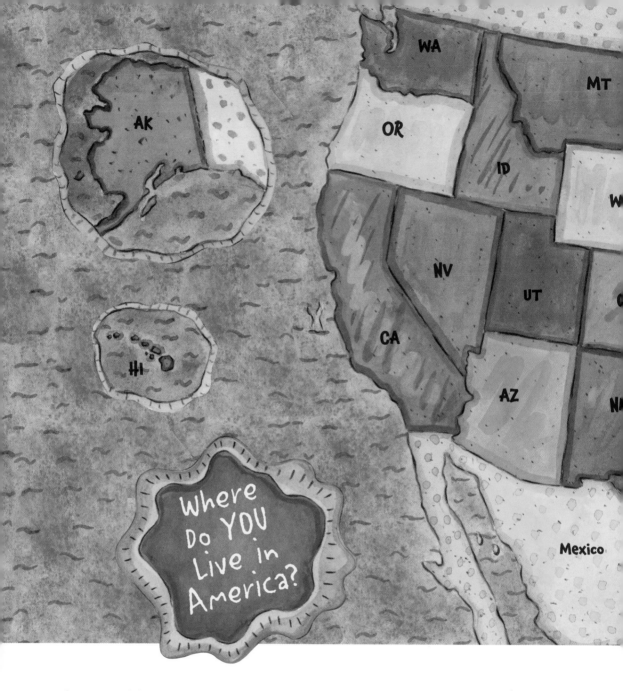

WA
MT
AK
OR
ID
W
NV
UT
CA
AZ
N
HI

Where Do YOU Live in America?

Mexico

Your address, state, town/city, and phone number:

4

Your favorite thing about America is:

WRITE!

Today's date: _____

_____

_____

_____

_____

_____

_____

_____

_____

_____

_____

_____

_____

_____

_____

_____

_____

_____

DRAW!

Today's date: _____

The great country of America!

Are you an American kid?
How many national facts do
you already know? See if you
can fill in the right answers!
(The correct answers are at the bottom
on the next page.)

National tree:

_____

National flower:

_____

National bird:

_____

National dance:

_____

National colors:

_____

National anthem:

National flag:

National motto:

Nation's first president:

National capital:

WRITE!

Today's date: _____

_____

_____

_____

_____

_____

_____

_____

_____

_____

_____

_____

_____

_____

_____

_____

_____

_____

DRAW!

Today's date: _____

Today we went to

_____

_____

_____

_____

My favorite thing about today was

_____

_____

_____

_____

_____

_____

_____

16

My least favorite thing about today was

Would I visit here again? Why or why not?

WRITE!

Today's date: _____

_____

_____

_____

_____

_____

_____

_____

_____

_____

_____

_____

_____

_____

_____

DRAW!

Today's date: _____

From apples to pineapples, America grows it all!

The wide range of temperatures in the US allows a lot of different types of fruit to grow. Washington, Michigan, and New York are filled with apple orchards, while states such as Georgia and South Carolina grow tasty peaches. California  is not only home to beautiful grape vineyards, but also strawberry fields, along with Florida, Oregon, and North Carolina. And of course, we cannot forget the Florida orange and the Hawaiian pineapple!

With all of this delicious fruit, you can make a colorful fruit salad! Just wash or peel your favorite fruits; cut them (with a grown-up's help) into bite-sized pieces; put them in a bowl and mix. Share with your favorite "fruity" friends.

For a tasty addition, toss in nuts or a few marshmallows!

What is your favorite kind of fruit?

Find out what kind of fruit grows in your state and plan a day picking fresh fruit. Perhaps you'll pick apples, strawberries, or peaches. (What about a peck of pickled peppers like Peter Piper picked?) Remember to bring a pail with you and collect enough fruit to make a famous American apple pie, strawberry jam, peach cobbler, blueberry muffins, or to even eat the fruit straight from the pail.

Have you ever picked fruit from an orchard or gone berry picking?

_____

_____

_____

What is your favorite fruit muffin?

_____

_____

_____

23

_____

_____

WRITE!

Today's date: _____

_____

_____

_____

_____

_____

_____

_____

_____

_____

_____

_____

_____

_____

_____

_____

_____

DRAW!

Today's date: _____

The proud symbol of America: Old Glory!

Today, the American flag, nicknamed Old Glory, contains 50 stars and 13 alternating stripes, seven red and six white. The stars represent the 50 states of the union, and the stripes represent the 13 original colonies. The national colors of red, white, and blue are especially symbolic as well. Red represents hardiness and valor, white symbolizes purity and innocence, and blue signifies vigilance, perseverance, and justice. Old Glory is a treasured symbol of America's proud past and promising future.

If you were to design a flag to symbolize you, what would it look like?

28

Make your own patriotic wind sock!

What you will need:

- 1 cylinder-shaped oatmeal box with the top and the bottom cut out
- Blue and white construction paper
- Red and white crepe paper streamers
- Hole punch   • Scissors   • Glue   • String

1. Cover the box with blue construction paper.

2. Using white paper, cut out several stars and glue them to the oatmeal box. Glue red and white streamers to one end of the box.

3. On the opposite end, punch four holes in the box.

4. Cut two pieces of string about a foot long and tie one string between two holes, sort of like you are tying on two handles.

Tie another piece of foot-long string to the "handles" to connect them. This last string is what you will use to tie your patriotic wind sock to a porch or tree branch.

29

WRITE!

Today's date: _____

_____

_____

_____

_____

_____

_____

_____

_____

_____

_____

_____

_____

_____

_____

DRAW!

Today's date: _____

Let's play some games!

Going on a trip?

Here are some fun games to play
on your next road trip.

Scavenger Hunt

Before you start out on your trip, make a list of items and places you
might see along the way (11 blue cars, 2 bridges, 5 motels, 3 towns that
have 10 letters in their names, etc.). Check them off as you find them.

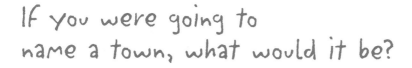

What is the funniest town name you've ever heard?

_____

_____

_____

_____

_____

If you were going to name a town, what would it be?

_____

_____

License Plate Game

Make a list of all the states. See how many different state license plates you can find, and check them off your list. (Variation: Keep a list of all the vanity plates you find.)

Make up your own funny license plates.

Auto Tag

Each person chooses a symbol or something you are likely to encounter regularly on the road, such as a gas station logo, a restaurant sign, a farm animal, a motorcycle. When a player sees her item, she calls it out and gently tags the next player, who then proceeds to search for his symbol, and so on.

35

WRITE!

Today's date: _____

_____

_____

_____

_____

_____

_____

_____

_____

_____

_____

_____

_____

_____

_____

DRAW!

Today's date: _____

Today we went to

_____

_____

_____

_____

My favorite thing about today was

_____

_____

_____

_____

_____

_____

_____

_____

_____

40

My least favorite thing about today was

Would I visit here again? Why or why not?

WRITE!

Today's date: _____

_____

_____

_____

_____

_____

_____

_____

_____

_____

_____

_____

_____

_____

_____

_____

DRAW!

Today's date: _____

Let's GROW something!

Grow a Pizza Garden!

Start plants indoors in early spring, then transfer to pots or the ground outside once they've sprouted and there is no longer danger of frost.

You'll need to grow:

HERBS:

- basil and oregano

VEGETABLES for SAUCE and TOPPINGS:

- tomatoes and bell peppers

The Chicago- and New York-Style Pizza

America took the idea of the pizza and made it its own, originating from the famous Chicago-style pizza and New York-style pizza. The Chicago-style pizza is a deep dish pizza three inches deep with a buttery crust, filled with lots of cheese and sauce. The New York-style pizza is wide with a thin crust and is usually eaten by folding the slice in half! Survey your friends and family and see if they have a favorite pizza style.

46

...Now...Let's COOK something!

Making a homemade pizza!

FOR YOUR CRUST:

You can use your favorite pizza-dough recipe, or a store-bought pizza crust, or even English muffin halves or tortillas for your crust.

MAKING FRESH PIZZA SAUCE:

Wash and cut as many tomatoes as you like into chunks.
Wash and dry a good handful each of basil and oregano, and chop.

In a saucepan over medium heat, sauté chopped onion and garlic in a small amount of butter or vegetable oil. If you like your sauce spicy, add crushed red pepper next. Now add the tomatoes and herbs and allow the mixture to come to a boil. Turn down the heat to a simmer, stirring occasionally, and let the sauce simmer until most of the liquid has cooked out.

Take sauce off the stove and use either a container blender or a hand-held blender to purée the sauce. Put sauce back on the heat, let it come to a boil again, then allow to simmer until it is the consistency you like.

Let it cool, then spread on pizza dough, or store in the fridge for another time.

ASSEMBLING YOUR PIZZA:

Spread sauce over pizza dough. Top with your chopped, fresh-picked peppers, and any other fresh veggies or meats you like. Now sprinkle cheese over everything and bake in the oven according to your pizza dough recipe. Yum! A homegrown pizza!

47

WRITE!

Today's date: _____

_____

_____

_____

_____

_____

_____

_____

_____

_____

_____

_____

_____

_____

_____

_____

_____

DRAW!

Today's date: _____

When it rains,
my favorite things to do:

_____

_____

_____

_____

_____

_____

_____

_____

_____

_____

favorite movie

_____

_____

_____

favorite TV show

_____

_____

_____

favorite video game

_____

_____

_____

favorite book

_____

_____

_____

favorite art projects

_____

_____

_____

WRITE!

Today's date: _____

_____

_____

_____

_____

_____

_____

_____

_____

_____

_____

_____

_____

_____

DRAW!

Today's date: _____

Today we went to

My favorite thing about today was

58

My least favorite thing about today was

_____

_____

_____

_____

_____

_____

_____

_____

Would I visit here again? Why or why not?

_____

_____

_____

_____

_____

_____

WRITE!

Today's date: _____

_____

_____

_____

_____

_____

_____

_____

_____

_____

_____

_____

_____

_____

_____

DRAW!

Today's date: _____

Today we went to

_____

_____

_____

_____

My favorite thing about today was

_____

_____

_____

_____

_____

_____

_____

_____

_____

My least favorite thing about today was

_____

_____

_____

_____

_____

Would I visit here again? Why or why not?

_____

_____

_____

_____

_____

WRITE!

Today's date: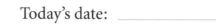

DRAW!

Today's date: _____

Let's play MORE GAMES!

Billboard Poetry

1. Take turns choosing four words from road signs.
2. Give those words to another player who will have one minute to turn the words into a four-line rhyming poem using one word per line.

Eating the Alphabet Game

To start, the first player says, "I'm so hungry I could eat an apple" (or anteater, or alligator). The second player then has to choose something beginning with the next letter of the alphabet, adding to the first player's choice: "I'm so hungry I could eat an apple and a balloon," and so on. See if your family can make it to Z, with each player remembering all the items that came before: "apple, balloon...zebra!"

What is your favorite food?

_____

_____

70

_____

_____

Can you think of some of your own fun games to play?

_____

_____

_____

_____

_____

_____

_____

_____

_____

_____

WRITE!

Today's date: _____

_____

_____

_____

_____

_____

_____

_____

_____

_____

_____

_____

_____

_____

_____

_____

DRAW!

Today's date: _____

Today we went to

_____

_____

_____

_____

My favorite thing about today was

_____

_____

_____

_____

_____

_____

_____

_____

My least favorite thing about today was

Would I visit here again? Why or why not?

WRITE!

Today's date: _____

_____

_____

_____

_____

_____

_____

_____

_____

_____

_____

_____

_____

_____

_____

_____

DRAW!

Today's date: _____

Let's go CAMPING in the American outdoors

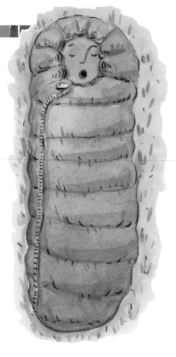

Mountains, canyons, deserts, forests, oceans, and lakes characterize America's natural and breathtaking landscape. The Rocky Mountains run through the American West, while the Appalachian Mountains run down the eastern part of the country. Desert areas cover the American Southwest while forests and lakes can be found in the North. America is home to a number of national parks, such as Yellowstone, Olympic, the Everglades, Acadia, and the Grand Canyon.

Have you ever gone camping? These national parks are wonderful places for you and your family to go for a camping trip! But until then, you can go camping in your own backyard...

Write about your camping experiences, or where you hope to go camping someday.

Outside and Inside S'mores

You'll need

Marshmallows
Graham crackers, broken in halves
Chocolate bars, broken in halves
A long stick or skewer for campfire s'mores, or
a baking sheet and aluminum foil for indoor s'mores

HOW TO MAKE CAMPFIRE S'MORES

Get your graham crackers and chocolate ready first.
Lay a chocolate bar half on one graham cracker half and have another
graham cracker half ready to go. Now put a marshmallow on the end of
your stick and hold over the fire, turning to keep it browning nicely and
evenly on all sides. It's finished when it's brown all over and a little crispy
on the outside. Now have a friend sandwich the marshmallow between
the graham and chocolate halves while you pull your stick out of the
marshmallow. Now you have a s'more!

HOW TO MAKE S'MORES IN THE OVEN

Heat oven to 350 degrees. Line a baking sheet with foil. Lay cracker
halves on baking sheet, top with chocolate bar halves, then marshmallows.
Toast in oven for about 5 minutes, just until marshmallow is melty and
chocolate begins to soften. Remove from oven and top with another
graham cracker half. S'mores indoors all year round!

WRITE!

Today's date: _____

_____

_____

_____

_____

_____

_____

_____

_____

_____

_____

_____

_____

_____

_____

_____

DRAW!

Today's date: _____

When I grow up I want to be

_____

_____

_____

_____

_____

_____

_____

_____

_____

_____

_____

_____

_____

_____

_____

A place I hope to go someday

WRITE!

Today's date: _____

_____

_____

_____

_____

_____

_____

_____

_____

_____

_____

_____

_____

_____

_____

_____

_____

DRAW!

Today's date: _____

If I wrote a book it would be about

_____

_____

_____

_____

_____

_____

_____

_____

_____

94

If I made a movie, it would be about

_____

_____

_____

If I made a TV show, it would be about

_____

_____

_____

If I could star in a movie, I would star as a

_____

_____

_____

If I could star in a TV show, I would star as a

_____

_____

_____

I think it would be fun to be an actor because

_____

_____

WRITE!

Today's date: _____

_____

_____

_____

_____

_____

_____

_____

_____

_____

_____

_____

_____

_____

_____

DRAW!

Today's date: _____

Today we went to

_____

_____

_____

_____

My favorite thing about today was

_____

_____

_____

_____

_____

_____

_____

_____

My least favorite thing about today was

_____

_____

_____

_____

_____

_____

_____

_____

Would I visit here again? Why or why not?

_____

_____

_____

_____

_____

_____

WRITE!

Today's date: _____

_____

_____

_____

_____

_____

_____

_____

_____

_____

_____

_____

_____

_____

_____

DRAW!

Today's date: _____

What do you love about going back to school?

106

School days

My favorite subject in school

_____

_____

_____

My least favorite subject in school

_____

_____

_____

If I were a teacher, I would

_____

_____

_____

If I could change one thing about school, I would

_____

_____

_____

The thing I like most about school

_____

_____

_____

WRITE!

Today's date: _____

_____

_____

_____

_____

_____

_____

_____

_____

_____

_____

_____

_____

_____

_____

_____

_____

DRAW!

Today's date: _____

WRITE!

Today's date: _____

_____

_____

_____

_____

_____

_____

_____

_____

_____

_____

_____

_____

_____

_____

_____

A place I hope to go someday

_____

_____

_____

If I could live anywhere in the world I'd choose

_____

_____

_____

Someone I wish lived near me

_____

_____

_____

Of all the places I've been, I liked this best

_____

_____

_____

Of all the places I've been, I really didn't like

_____

_____

_____

If I could change one thing
about where I live it would be

_____

_____

_____

_____

_____

_____

_____

_____

_____

WRITE!

Today's date: _____

_____

_____

_____

_____

_____

_____

_____

_____

_____

_____

_____

_____

_____

_____

DRAW!

Today's date: _____

Can you write your own poem? Here's how.

1st Stanza

I am... (*two special characteristics you have*)

I wonder .... (*something you are actually curious about*)

I hear... (*an imaginary sound*)

I see.. (*an imaginary sight*)

I want.. (*an actual desire*)

I am..................................... (*the first line of the poem repeated*)

2nd Stanza

I pretend................................... (*something you actually pretend to do*)

I feel .... (*a feeling about something imaginary*)

I touch... (*an imaginary touch*)

I worry .... (*something that really bothers you*)

I cry............................... (*something that makes you very sad*)

I am........................... (*the first line of the poem repeated*)

3rd Stanza

I understand .... (*something you know is true*)

I say.. (*something you believe in*)

I dream................................. (*something you actually dream about*)

I try................................(*something you really make an effort about*)

I hope....................................... (*something you actually hope for*)

I am...................................... (*the first line of the poem repeated*)

Now, write your own poem here:

1st Stanza

I am _____

I wonder _____

I hear_____

I see _____

I want_____

I am _____

2nd Stanza

I pretend_____

I feel_____

I touch _____

I worry_____

I cry _____

I am _____

3rd Stanza

I understand _____

I say _____

I dream _____

I try _____

I hope_____

I am _____

121

WRITE!

Today's date: _____

_____

_____

_____

_____

_____

_____

_____

_____

_____

_____

_____

_____

_____

_____

_____

_____

DRAW!

Today's date: _____

Do you know the city of our nation's first capital? Philadelphia — the city of brotherly love and...soft pretzels!

Before Washington D.C. became the national capital and home to the White House, Philadelphia, Pennsylvania claimed the title for ten years. Home not only to Benjamin Franklin, the city also boasts such monuments as the Liberty Bell and Independence Hall, where the Declaration of Independence was believed to be signed. But in the early 1800s Washington D.C. was chosen as the US capital. Maybe if you visit, you'll see the president and his family in the White House where they live.

Although it is no longer our nation's capital, Philadelphia still holds reminders of its important past, and it is also proud of its famous soft pretzels. Let's make some!

Other city nicknames you may know

Detroit, Michigan
The Motor City

Boston, Massachusetts
Beantown

Denver, Colorado
The Mile High City

New York, New York
The Big Apple

St. Louis, Missouri
Gateway to the West

Chicago, Illinois
The Windy City

Make your own soft pretzel!

Ingredients:
- 1 tbsp. yeast
- ½ c. warm water
- 1 tsp. honey
- 1¼ cup white whole wheat flour
- ½ tsp. salt

Directions:

1. Put the yeast in a small bowl with the water and honey. Stir, and then let the mixture sit for about 5 minutes.

2. Mix 1 cup of flour and salt together.

3. After the 5 minutes is up, check on the yeast mixture. It should be bigger than before and a little bubbly. Add this mixture to the flour and salt mixture.

4. Stir everything together. Use a spoon to start, but finish with your hands. The dough is ready when it is still a little crumbly and flaky. Gradually add more flour if mixture is too wet and sticky.

5. Put the dough on the cutting board and knead it into one big ball.

6. Break off a piece of dough that's about the size of a large marble. Use your hands to roll it into a skinny snake.

7. Twist the snake into a medium-size pretzel shape, and put it on the cookie sheet. Do this with all the dough, making 12 pretzels. For a variation sprinkle unbaked pretzels with cinnamon and sugar.

8. Bake your pretzels for 10 minutes at 325° Fahrenheit. Let them cool and enjoy!

What makes YOU an American kid?